# A CERTAIN ATTITUDE:
## Poems by Seven Texas Women

# A CERTAIN ATTITUDE:
## Poems by Seven Texas Women

edited by Laura B. Kennelly

Pecan Grove Press
San Antonio, Texas

ISBN: 1-877603-28-7

Pecan Grove Press
Box AL
1 Camino Santa Maria
San Antonio, Texas 78228-8608

Acknowledgment is due the following journals and anthologies where some of these poems first appeared:

SuAnne Doak: ● *New Mexico Humanities Review*, "No Way Out" ●*RiverSedge*, "Horses," "Just at Dawn" ● *Concho River Review*, "Delayed Response" ● *RE:Arts & Letters*, "Swallows" ● *New Texas '92*, "West Texas Ghost Lights"

Lynn Hoggard: ● *Travois*, "A Learning," "Litany" ● *Helios*, "Poetry as Lemon" ● *New Texas '91*, "Vampire Girl" ● *Concho River Review*, "Kaleidoscope in White"

Laura Kennelly: ● *RiverSedge*, "Delta Ladies," "Testament" ● *New Texas '92*, "Pre-Op" ● *RE:Arts & Letters*, "Flash Flood" ● *Concho River Review*, "Esperar lo imposible" ● *April Perennial, Dog River Review*, "Hamlets" ● *San José Studies*, "Helen with Insomnia, at the Clavier," "Lara to Zhivago" ● *A Measured Response*, "Clytemnestra Junior in Detroit" ● *Tin Wreath*, "Yard Report"

Vicky Lee Santiesteban: ● *Madison Review*, "Sightings" ● *RiverSedge*, "Pan," "My Babylon" ● *Denny Poems*, "My Babylon"

Sheryl St. Germain: ● *RE: Arts & Letters*, "Dallas Texas: Not From a Native Daughter" ● *How Heavy the Breath of God*, "In the Garden of Eden" ● *Cream City Review*, "My Body in Summer" ● *The Massachusetts Review*, "Pain Killers" ● *Abiko Quarterly*, "Keeping the Roses Alive" ● *On the Bus*, "Hacking Away the Wisteria"

Frances M. Treviño: ● *Grasslands Review*, "To You Who Leave San Antonio"

# Introduction

If you're looking for some cowgirl poetry—some female version of what is ordinarily thought of as "Texas poetry," full of images of livestock, barbed wire, mesquite, and branding irons—just close the book. There's not a longhorn or a fence post to be found here.

That is not to say there are no poems about place, about living and breathing and eating and loving in the state of Texas. In "To You Who Leave San Antonio," for instance, Frances M. Treviño describes her native city as "Colored warm with stripes," a place where "Even the blues are orange." In another of her poems, South Texas appears as existing "in the whirlwind of / Grain and salt / Where horizon and landscape / Mesh into the only / Texas sunsets in the world." SuAnne Doak's "West Texas Ghost Lights" revolves around the mysterious Marfa lights of the state's folklore, and Texas weather makes its appearance in Laura Kennelly's "Yard Report" and Lynn Hoggard's "Torrid Heat." And no one captures the details and the ambiance of Texas better than Sheryl St. Germain, in her poem "Dallas, Texas: Not from a Native Daughter":

> But it is this, if truth be told, that keeps us here,
> not that the lemon blue sky, as unending as milk, is not
> tempting, or the clusters of mesquite, or the flowering
> in spring and summer, but maybe there is something stubborn
> and American about this unshapeliness, this bounty, this
> half-digested wisdom, the fearless stupid intelligence
> that believes anything to be possible: again, the frontier.

Some of the place-oriented poems reflect the fact that Texas is simultaneously a western and a southern state, and that many of its citizens identify more with the South than with the West. The persona of Treviño's poem "Southern and in Detroit" admits that "now, more than ever / I think I miss the South." Certainly no poem could claim to be more southern than Kennelly's "Delta Ladies," with its gossipy, rain-soaked, sugar-voiced, bourbon-drinking females. And no Yankee-born or desert-bred poet could handle with such dexterity the "wanton, exuberant, triumphant, almost hysterical" wisteria in St. Germain's poem "Hacking Away the Wisteria."

Still, such "regional," place-dependent poems are in the minority. These seven native daughters appear more interested in poetic explorations of people than of place. Elemental emotions like fear, pain, hunger, love, hate, and anger permeate the lines about relationships—between lovers or betrayers (of either sex), between friends, between children and adults (parents or otherwise).

Some of the poets cast their messages about human interaction in nets woven of the myths, legends, folklore, and literature of the past. As evident in her titles, literary and mythological allusions are particularly abundant in Kennelly's poems: "Helen with Insomnia, at the Clavier," "Clytemnestra Junior in Detroit," "Lara to Zhivago." Referring to the old stories helps the poet illuminate the continuities existing between ancient history and today's events: "Bad news is always the same; only a few changes / in a few thousand years," Kennelly claims in one poem, reminding readers that the behavior and motivations of the gods and goddesses, heroes and heroines, villains and sinners of yesterday can still be seen amidst the chaos of the twentieth century. Giuli Coniglio's prose poem creates a believable voice for Scheherazade, the narrator of the *Arabian Nights*: "To make a long story short, *she began*, was not the point, has never been the point." Referring to more contemporary literature, Doak mentions poet William Stafford in her poem "No Absolution" and creates a whole new way to think about Anne Sexton in her "Aunt Sadie Talking About Anne Sexton."

Other poems rely less on classical, Western-world allusions and turn instead to ancient symbolism. Goddess-feminist and earth-mother images appear in Hoggard's incantatory "Litany," for example, describing the earth mother's hair as "the greying musk of moss / trailing loose from oak tree to the earth," her arms as "branches of a naked tree / rotting in an upward stretch," and her belly as "the swamp / where womb consumes what it creates." Rather than describing her from a distance, the poet/persona in St. Germain's "My Body in Summer" actually becomes an earth goddess: "I am a feast, / a garden, a corpse, / my skin suckled and flayed, / . . . this odoriferous perfume, / this blessed sweating body." Coniglio's darkly clever "Iron John's Nightmare" seems at first to be about a woman's fear of meeting a "gluttonous and bloody" Robert Bly-type wild man, but a twist in the last stanza makes it clear that whatever rage and violence is about to occur will emanate from the "ravening jaws" of the female rather than from the male.

Women's bodies are not the only ones objectified in this

collection. Kennelly's Helen laments that the object of her affection is beyond her reach, "but just once," she says, "I'd like to strip that plumed / helmet off his head, loosen the armor plate, / touch his skin and bring him to fevers." Treviño boasts of what she'll do to her favorite sexual object in "The Indian of My Dreams":

> And if he can withstand
> The wrath of my fire crown
> Claws on my hands and feet
> Badness in me
> Then he can embrace the energy of
> Any mountain, ocean or desert
> And I would climb the pyramids of Tenochtitlan
> Again and again and again
> In honor of my worthy warrior.

Hoggard's Vampire Girl admits of her tryst with her vampire lover: "I could kill for this! / could drop house, car / all my friends / to crawl on my belly / back into this swamp!" Vicky Santiesteban's poem "The Seraphs of Spain" is filled with sensuous details about a summer relationship enjoyed by two men and one woman. "When the music ends, the friend / bows backwards and Antonio kisses him on the mouth / looking at me as if he hopes I will be offended," she writes. In the last stanza of this poem, the lightheartedness of the previous six turns serious, the image an echo of the voracious earth-mothers in the poems of Hoggard, St. Germain, and Coniglio:

> I am on my knees in a vineyard when a dark haired
> angel lets a slow trickle of wine wash over my face,
> warming my neck, and I am drunk with excitement
> knowing that later I will digest him.

As willing as these poets are to express the reckless pleasure of total abandonment to passion, they are also willing to describe the potential perils. "For you I will take off / clothes, rings, consciousness / and go into the dark," says Kennelly in "Pre-Op"; in "Esperar lo imposible," she explores the entanglements of the mind brought on by the entanglements of the flesh: "Love inexorably alters my world; would / it could not. Yet still my body reaches, / searches each morning for yours." Hoggard voices a similar sentiment in the oft-repeated line "Love's sorrows sear the heart in bitter pain," in "Plaisirs D'Amour." St. Germain's

"Sestina to the Beloved" explores the pain of loving someone who does not desire the same level of commitment:

> What I want is uncompromising, what I want
> is difficult,
> is like wanting water to offer breath,
> is like wanting fire to undress
> itself, is about possession undressing
> itself, is about what it means to be speaking
> at all, is about belonging like breath
> to the beloved, the one whose bones
> are inside you like so many difficult
> hearts, the only one you want to want

That loving opens the heart to pain is also evident in the poems exploring the complex relationship between children and adults, whether told from the adult's or the child's point of view. Treviño notes the irony of women who "hold the babies / who will love them / in the unconditional way / which their / boyfriends and husbands / do not." More poignantly, Hoggard speaks of the desire to "reach to all the ones I love / who rush past me / blowing kisses, waving goodbye / Nothing I do can save them / Nothing can save me / from the terror of their beauty." Santiesteban's "My Babylon," a masterful exploration of a father/daughter relationship, begs for love ("Oh, Papa. Oh, my pretty Papa. Make me good") at the same time it accepts the guilt for *and* blames the shadowy adult figure for taking advantage of a child's trust:

> I didn't mean to frighten him. I only knew too much to ever want to leave my bed. It was easier there. Still, the dark was a cruel place to keep me. He must have known that. I said it so many times.

Her frightened child-voice in "Sightings" also knows that "You can lose the things you love a lot of ways." A similar knowledge is obvious in Doak's poem about watching the nightly news, with its images of "Iraqi faces sealed with grief, / holding their dead children," and "in the dark, an old woman / humming a grandchild / into unharmed sleep, / while chemicals spread / like a benediction."

That these poets acknowledge the anxiety and anguish of life does not mean that they have no sense of humor. "French Pastry" by Hoggard, told from a streetwalker's point of view, is divided into "Tart 1" and "Tart 2" and uses well-known tourist attractions to symbolize both male and female genitalia: "My

Paris, huge with love / your *Tour Eiffel* / my *Arc de Triomphe*." In "The Transfiguration of Louisa Mari," Coniglio tells the story of a woman who cooks so much that she has to put a second oven in her basement. Her friends and family are puzzled at her obsession with going up and down the stairs while cooking delicious meals, but they decide the results were "extremely invigorating" and they "equated meals at her house with sex, or skinny-dipping." Treviño's "mother" in "My Mother Who Burns Tortillas" insists on making eggs and tortillas every Sunday even though she's a terrible cook. Every time, "the poor tortilla, being subjected / to level seven heat, begins to blacken." And if you can read without laughing St. Germain's description of the native Texas male who "sounds like he's got a half- / ate boiled egg in his mouth when he talks," then you've never been to Texas.

The poems in this collection explore on all levels what it means to be female, to play out one's life in a world at best indifferent and at worst hostile toward girls and women. The poets have not shied away from discussions of uncomfortable subjects: resentment, lust, incest, fear, child abuse. Yet these are not, for the most part, whiny or angry poems. They are simply "learnings," responses to the complexity of being born, growing up, and growing old, as a female.

—Charlotte M. Wright
Denton, Texas
October 1994

Charlotte M. Wright is currently the editor of the University of North Texas Press, and was formerly assistant editor of *Western American Literature.* Her chapbook from the Redneck Press is titled *Crazy Horse and Walt Whitman's Hands.*

# Contents

## Lynn Hoggard

## Laura Kennelly

## Vicky Lee Santiesteban

## Sheryl St. Germain

## Frances M. Treviño

Giuli Coniglio was educated at Rice, Cornell, and Kansas universities and received her master's degree from the University of North Texas. She has taught both middle school and college level English, and currently works as a freelance writer and copy editor.

## Upon Surviving Her Husband, Scheherazade Explains Herself

—To make a long story short, *she began*, was not the point, has never been the point. After all, he desired a story, came expressly for the story; so if I had hurried my tale, had left out all the clearly interesting parts—for example, if I had not mentioned that the thief escaped into a large pit of snakes, if the thief had simply escaped, if there had been no pit, no snakes—that would have ended all his pleasure, the story would not have created an urge to go on. Just as the boy, who kept finding treasures buried under each spot of earth that the peacock pecked the moment the moon appeared on the horizon, went on, day after day, promising to quit his quest when the peacock proved wrong, when the treasure could not be found, even though he dug beneath the peacock's spot in ever widening circles, further and further from the center, far beyond the starting point, until he found some likely trifle to prove the peacock right, to give him a reason to watch for the peacock again the following evening, and the evening after that . . . if I had not pursued that part of the story—well, the story would not have satisfied. So you see, it was more than my own ending I attempted to postpone, more than my own fear that kept me telling tales. Perhaps it was the moon, or the pleasure, the peacock, the treasure, the hopeful boy; I am sorry only that the man did not last as long as they.

## The Transfiguration of Louisa Mari

Cooking was her passion, so she cooked all the time;
had to get a second oven—in the basement.
The Sears man looked surprised, until she explained:
*It's cool down there—now the upstairs will stay cool.*

Her middle-aged offspring attempted to intervene (for her health);
she countered *It's too much trouble to move the oven upstairs,*
and continued to cook on two levels, to go up and down
and up and down—down for veal cutlets, up for broccoli.

Having mastered all her favorite dishes, Louisa
quickly added more to her tandem repertoire.
A dinner guest, impressed by her culinary agility,
remarked *Louisa's dinners exhibit deft coquereography.*

Guests rated her repasts extremely invigorating.
(They equated meals at her house with sex, or skinny-dipping.)
She relished every chance she had for inspired improvisation;
garnished plates with crispy manna, topped ice cream with
    ambrosia ribbons.

Louisa, becoming light on her feet, dipped and whirled
between kitchen and basement, evanesced across the floor,
bringing sustenance to enraptured guests, who frequently noticed,
while in her presence, their own or a neighbor's phosphorescence.

## Trout Lines

Quite proud of his fishes, threaded through the jaws
with lines invisible to distant eyes,
each man assumes the same, sated smile,
parenthesized by dimpled cheeks.  You tell
them apart by their hats, or in one case,

the lack of a hat.  Hatless, a bald man
exhibits the biggest fishes.  His hands rest
lightly on the lucid filament
connecting each fish to all the others.
They frame his catch as if to say, "These are mine.

These are *my* fine fish, that I caught with sun
assailing my uncovered head—obstinate
as I am, I refuse to wear a hat."
Other men—in paperboy caps, crumpled
fedoras, even a stiff, straw one, brimmed—

with smaller catches dangling for display,
stand behind, behind the transparent strand,
not daring to share someone else's prize.

## There Are No Monets in the Louvre

I see the world opaquely most days, faces of people
I used to know appearing on shoulders of bus drivers,
postal carriers; still these myopic pools surprise me,

let me see through them occasionally to recognize
translucence in the mystery of the hidden picture,
even without clarifying spectacles.

I imagine it's like looking, twice, at a Monet
*dans le Louvre*, majestically appropriating an end wall;
up close the colors are *it*, lacking shape, stirring senses

alone, dizzying vision. But standing back, head tilted,
mouth agape, fishlike, distinct forms surface—lily pads,
grassy meadows—the impressionistic haze precipitating

wonder. *How'd I miss them? Where were they?* Opening
to question . . . well, if they were just colors after all,
or if imperfect vision distorted them, covered them temporarily.

# A Muse-Lover's Quarrel

You kept on slamming doors, mixed honeyed phrases
with crystallized endings, threw your zestless words
my way.  All I could do was read, alone,
intent on Milton, waiting for a right,
silent moment (the air devoid of all
your raving but still tinted with your leaving),
the time to retaliate with my words, my
own argument. It came. I began, but

the words seemed mute; no voice breathed inside them.
Mere gestures, Chaplin-like, were all I made.
Then suddenly, I found myself waking
from heavy sleep. The quarrel we had fading,
my fingers kneaded deep impressions of books—
disfiguring red furrows—from my face.

## The Monolith, Observed

A stonefaced man looks inland, rigid
back to the pounding tide that changes
slowly, but changes nonetheless, whether
or not he chooses to confront its steady
progress.  He laughs, and simply disregards
the force pushing him forward, or backward,
still further in.  Soon,

you'll feel his gaze, even in sleep.
You might try dislodging those glowing,
crimson eyes, try leaving them lying
there, upturned in the wet sand,
but the empty sockets, steel-gray,
would still suggest red, coral-
edged eyes, staring.  See

how he cradles his bulging belly—as if
suppressing a laugh.  A shadow lingers
at the base of his neck, looks three-
dimensional, concave—an inviting
chasm for a careful blade—a petroglyph
etched by sun.  A finger placed
just so could topple him.  How

might he sound, then?—his cold
face pressed against the ground, a foot
wedged in the small of his back, his exposed
flesh blistered, someone else's hot
breath whispering *Laugh now.*

## Nom de Guerre

My father's family comes from Sicily.
He gave me a name—echo of his own,
with fewer syllables—and yet, in tone,
rhythm, and sound, it flaunts heredity.
The locals speak my name so carelessly,
it often makes me wonder if they've known,
in their fixed lives, that cultures not their own
exist—no, *thrive*—down the street, across the sea.

Still, I harbor domestic sentiments.
Although paternal voices urge me toward
revenge upon *paesano* ignorance,
maternal manners, the Puritan cord,
secure patience, restrain my rabid mood;
my smile becomes an executioner's hood.

## Bus to Palestine

I saw this scraggly guy stumbling toward me,
his lashless, blue-white, wild dog stare fixed right
on me, or maybe my window.  Afraid
he'd want to fight if he caught me watching,

I glanced, sort of sideways, out the edge of
my eyes.  I thought he'd seen; I pretended
the girl's curly red hair tumbled over
the seat ahead was my object, wondered

just how long one glossy strand would be, pulled
taut, how long I could pull before she'd turn,
how long he'd keep them hard blue-aggies aimed
at me, what the world might look like, seen through

the white swirl of those hypnotic marbles.
Transparent flames rose up from the pavement
ahead. The guy's cool breath, like smoke, curled round
my shoulder.  Then a pair of hands, scissors,

a falling ribbon of glossy red hair,
a closing fist—I turned to look, I pried
his fingers up one at a time (*the red-
head had not turned*) and spied a delicate

ruby-throated hummingbird perched on his
palm, flying out my half-opened window.
I felt a whirring hover inside, risked
a look straight in his eyes, found cloud and sky.

## Clearing Corners

*It is the Past's supreme italic*
*Makes this Present mean—*
—Emily Dickinson

In corners, gathered so you'd never look,
lie relics from my shyer days:

a pair of leather shoes—outdated, drab,
yet weathered, scant-heeled, overused;

old hats that hid my face from prying eyes,
their ample brims turned down too low;

torn photographs, stacked, old on top of new
(relations, strangers, scenes I might

have staged).  I've tried before to box them up,
to ditch those tag-alongs slowing my pace.

They're sly—they seem to settle in unnoticed,
then show up at my table (not

invited); wan and hopeful, like refugees.

## Iron John's Nightmare

The snap of his jaws, that knife-sharpening
slither of steely teeth, might be enough
to turn me back, wondering why I
belly-crawled this far through the brambles,
maneuvered around hidden quicksand,
leapt gracefully over that gaping pit
filled with glowing (but cold) bones—
the pit I had to go beyond to reach
the running stream, my destination.

It might be enough, I think.
And then I arrive, and there the beast
waits, as expected, parading himself,
patrolling the bank with shoulder-punching strides,
aiming slow-blinking looks (gluttonous and bloody)
my way, his tongue religiously tasting
teeth, anticipating his ritual feast,
his calculated, sacrificial kill,
the expression of his self-love.

Then I hear it—a deep, rolling bellow
reverberates from some ancient abyss.
I feel it ripple through my cowardly spine,
engulf me, jerk its hidden snare taut, catch
me, unaware.  I think he's in reach,
glance toward his pacing ground, discover
he's crossing the stream, abandoning watch,
the booming rumble radiating, now robust
and fluent, from my own ravening jaws.

SuAnne Doak teaches English at Cisco Junior College where she is Director of Development. She is currently working on a second novel.

## No Absolution

My daughter begs me
to stop after a cat's
innocent step onto pavement
is caught by a pickup
in the oncoming lane,
left twisting on asphalt.
How can I explain
that going back cannot
alter the turning
of wheels?
If only we could have
a moment like the one
in Stafford's poem
about the doe hit
by a car, an epiphany
of doing what's right
for everyone,
an act of compassion
to forgive us
for being alive.
But in the mirror
I see only traffic,
know my child
will not understand.

## Moths

On a night when desert air
was sodden with unfallen rain
they invaded the house
in kamikaze squadrons

crashing against lamps
and walls; we slapped at them
until the floor was stacked
and still they were swarming.

I could believe their maddened
urge to show the bastards
no matter how many times
they swat at you.

As rain finally happened,
we swept out dead moths—
wind tossing them like lint
into the wet dark.

Later, dreaming a carnage
of wings milky as bones,
I woke to the hugeness
of flutterings.

## No Way Out

In a windowless building,
outside winter a flat gray
fattening to green,
rain a solid pour—
a gully washer like those
that hurried my grandmother
to the center of the room
out of lightning reach.

It'll wash us away,
she'd moan, fish-eyeing
the ceiling for leaks
that lead to deluges.
Now, I look up,
wish for a flood and a raft—
mind's eyes unfolding
travel brochures,
scenarios hidden buds
bursting with great ideas.

The walls sneer like my neighbor
in the laundry room
shoving quarters into the slot,
her cigarette lip dangled
around what she tells
the truckers at the place
she works nights:
Fat chance.

# Entertainment Tonight

As if the latest celebrity
couplings are not trivial,
the television smile drones on.
But I'm thinking about
Iraqi faces sealed with grief,
holding their dead children,
nerve gas from the army
stopping the heartbeats
of their own people,
those left alive
abandoning cars and buses
like stranded fossils
on the highways out of Baghdad—
running, always running,
their shoes desperate
in sand impossible to walk on,
their used-up breaths
sputtering: Allah, save us!
sorrow a bundle carried
with their belongings,
their minds yearning with
each step for sun-crusted houses
soaking up evening's
cool immersion, an olive tree's
prayerful rustle
in the dark, an old woman
humming a grandchild
into unharmed sleep,
while chemicals spread
like a benediction.

# Horses

In the spindle eye
of morning,
their tails are shawls
fringing the air.

My daughter follows
the flow of their colors
like multi-hued water,
stroking the white one
in hopes that he will
leap the fence,
charmed as a unicorn.

Her small hands
grasp in her sleep
for the rough caress
of mane, her knees tense
to arch the wind
with flank and sinew.

Her dreams lighten her;
she jumps unafraid,
not noticing equine
features growing
human, and arms
embracing her
to the ride's end.

Someday, with a man
she loves, her touch
will smooth his body
as they hold steady,
take flight.

## Just at Dawn

What was that howling
at the edge of sleep—
a host of wolves,

their tongues huge enough
to smother you,
their breath

like a lover's,
panting *let us in.*
Stars complicating black

told you nothing,
the wind's lips
were sealed,

darkness taking with it
whatever demon
sent to bedevil you.

Or was it a pinprick
of time not yet
opened in the sky,

when your daughter
will leave you solitary
as that last star

trying to stay up
for the sun.        ·
Everywhere, old women

smocked in white beds
crochet prayers
with the heels

of their palms,
their mouths' wrinkled
paper smiling—yes,

we know you, we're
saving you a window
with a view.

## Delayed Response

White tails drift
across the pasture
toward the woods
and he is back
huddled in blankets,
smoke ammonia
up his nose, men
circling the fire,
goddamming themselves
awake, long barrels
elbow-crooked,
his father handing
him his first coffee cup.
In the deer stand
cold wrapping his feet,
he dozed until his reflexes
obeyed his father's: Shoot!
watched leap of gray
crumple, stretched out
his hand—not a tremble,
walked to meet
the round, glass eye.
Back at camp,
the knife ripped clean
as a surgeon,
steam like incense,
a hawk screaming overhead;
he turned away
from antlers laid out,
a sacrifice.
Now, he follows sleek flanks
into the trees,
brushes a hand
across his eyes.

## Swallows

They arrive with spring's
other excesses, driven
by the oldest of urges,

crapping up the porch,
and her father gets out
the .410, taking awkward aim

because of where he was sliced
through the breastbone—
a miss, and he hands her the gun.

Her eyesight is good, her reflexes
trigger the blunt recoil
ending in a blizzard

of polished blue feathers.
He nods, "Good shot!"
Her hair ripples like plumage

as they walk to where wings
no longer scissor the air.
Decades ago their flashlights

trailed a rattling to clever paws
shopping for garbage;
pillaging continued,

but there was no talk
of guns, just their laughter
at can lids tilted like hats

on mannequins. Today,
they do not talk about how close
he came to the last heartbeat

or the reasons for a swallow's death.
Feathers litter the ground.
He picks one up, turns it over:

"Pretty. Too bad they make
a mess"—lets it fall
like he did forget-me-nots

on her mother's coffin.
She takes his arm—now the one
who must deal with intruders.

## West Texas Ghost Lights

I'm telling him how
the Comanches called them
Ghost Lights, believed
they capture souls,
followed a safer path
coming up from Mexico,
but my skeptical friend
purses his mouth
around "swamp gas"
and "car lights,"
even though no highway
reaches south toward
the Chihuahuan Desert.
Then they appear,
fiery eyes burning
through dark thick
as wool, levitating over
ocatillo spears,
white-headed yucca,
parched air no swamp
could breathe in.
Once I drove at night
through opalescent fire
rising like prayers
from drowned animals,
fences, trees
as flood waters kissed
the lip of the road.
I felt the same
as I do tonight, east
of Marfa, sitting
on the hood of my friend's
pick-up, rich scent
of greasewood sensuous
as a lover's tongue.

What are they
these Roman candles
launched by no one?
My friend pops a beer,
asks what I'm talking
about—he doesn't
see anything.

## Aunt Sadie Talking About Anne Sexton

Darling, did you hear about the woman
who gave birth to an old man?  Such a life!
But, it happens.  Think about poor Anne.
Talk about psychological problems—I mean,
if you had a father who screwed you up,
you'd end up in the loony bin, too.
And even out in the boat, for godsakes.
She should have been making it with some
nice young guy, but when he takes off his pants,
who does he remind her of but the old fart?
Could you say to such a man: can we talk?
I tell you, not even if he were a rabbi.
So what else could she do?  She tried everything—
enemas, pills, the works—no abortion.
Imagine the embarrassment of so many failures.
Even her words she treated like a rape—slap
the nouns around, use a razor on verbs.
I say to you, precious, she should have talked
to me. I know how to handle such a schlemiel.
And then the boy thing.  Did I tell you what
happened?  She married him, even though
everybody kept telling her—don't do it,
the guy's a bum! But that Annie.  Stubborn.
Which is good only if it doesn't make you want
to pick out your own coffin.   Ach, such a waste.
She should have told him to go hit on
some other gentile poet and let the hell go
of her privates.  It's so simple.
But what does she do—heads straight for
the medicine cabinet.  He should have died
choking on his own vomit.  If God runs heaven,
he should.  Know what I mean?

Lynn Hoggard, a graduate of the University of Southern California, teaches French at Midwestern State University in Wichita Falls. Her translation of Paul Valéry's *Ébauche d'un serpent* as *Sketch of a Serpent* was published by Thorp Springs Press (1987).

## A Learning

Miz Boudreaux kept on beating
her held by the one left arm she grabbed
to yank her off the front porch swing
the four year old, she yelling
Evil chile, evil! sweet-singin'
about de devil an's to how you love 'im
Give you a learnin', devil chile!

She sang, dark Cajun woman
swinging back and forth a sure right arm
across the blonde-haired, bobbing form
whose cries were all of Sunday School
and loving even Satan-enemies
Now swelling for the world to hear

Where no one did
but a few black snakes
tucked in mud at the bayou's edge
that writhed, then opened
then closed dark heads
around a glimpse
of white.

## Litany

Your hair the greying musk of moss
trailing loose from oak tree to the earth
lair of spiders nest of squirrels
      my bed
oh earth mother my mother


Your arms the branches of a naked tree
rotting in an upward stretch
swaying to the rhythms of the slow earth chant
      swaying me
oh earth mother my mother


From your breasts the ceaseless rain
falling hot on fertile ground
calling chaos from the maddened vegetation
      hot on me
oh earth mother my mother


In your belly swarms the swamp
where womb consumes what it creates
perpetual birth, unending death
      my source
oh earth mother my mother


Your sons the rustling snakes
perfidious servants to your will
my brothers, lovers
      my life and death
oh earth mother my mother, my mother

## French Pastry

Tart 1.

I was a streetwalker then

but literal-minded
I took the streets of Paris
one by one, by two at night

My Paris, huge with love
your *Tour Eiffel*
my *Arc de Triomphe*
laced
by my dreaming footsteps

I was a sleepwalker then


Tart 2.

Other streetwalkers
stayed awake
and didn't move

The ones outside my flat
just leaned and looked
hungry

With openings for dreams
each Hélène drew Paris
through her doors

> *Viens ici, chéri*
> *tu verras des choses*
> *tu verras des choses*

## Poetry as Lemon

Freud said that art
sublimates and
is cathartic
Goethe blew out
Werther's brains,
not his

And now I've
written it all down
all about the frenzy and the itch
externalized; suffused; controlled

But when I put my pencil
down, my hand, I note
still
trembles

## Plaisirs D'Amour

The joys of love will dazzle like a flame
the one who circles, seeking its embrace
Love's sorrows sear the heart in bitter pain

He searches, restless with desire, to claim
his lover's touch, her scent, her hair, her face—
the joys of love that dazzle like a flame

He cries and begs her not to leave. In vain
he laughs and tries to snuff out every trace
of love that sears the heart in bitter pain

She slips into his dreams to call his name
and, teasing, disappears at his embrace
The joys of love keep dazzling like a flame

that spreads across his life and seams his brain
with wounds the world and time cannot erase
Love's sorrows sear the heart in bitter pain

while the song of love repeats its sweet refrain
and, dizzy, round he goes, caught in the chase,
The joys of love still dazzling like a flame
as sorrow sears the heart in bitter pain

## Torrid Heat

in a skillet
will crack the woody
cellulose of
okra, break it down
make it
lovable

and on a tennis court
in Texas summer
will steam
the seasoned soul
delicious

## Vampire Girl

*Tonight I open my window wide;*
*maybe he won't come.*

I lie dreaming I might slip away
but feel again the ache
of a wound being picked open
as he fits his teeth
into the socket on my neck

He's killing me, the no-count
but I don't cry out, don't cry
    die
    into amoeba
    ooze   and   pulse
    wave on wave of sweetness
    rolling
    through a one-celled universe

    Plashing
    sinking
    then leaping up
    a hook through my lip
    slick and sleek and rainbow-scaled
    I twist and shine in the sun!

    I could kill for this!
    could drop house,  car
    all my friends
    to crawl on my belly
    back into this swamp!

Sated, he rises
over my dead body and withers
into a black leather glove
that flaps off.
I lie dreaming
where I slipped
away.

## sub-rosa:

under the roses

underneath     underhand

    underwater

submarine

    seamen     semen

seawater     rose-water

    sub-rosa

sub-lunary     lunatic

sub-luminate

sublimate

rosy rosy sub-rosa love

## Guarding the Mystery

> *—the fire, the fire inside!*
> —John of the Cross

Deep in the soul
is a cave where someone kneels
mouthing sounds I cannot
understand. He speaks to a fire
mirrored in his eyes. I know
that what he does is the center
of everything important

The way began simply
with insomnia—the brain gone night-clubbing
again, the body cross and sharp-tongued
at being dragged from one silly image to another
When the pair would finally collapse across
some table, arms entwined, the soft tap-
tapping of the tiny mallet at the skull
would start again, the world
insisting to be let back in

It entered as a burning wood
guarded by a lion
Small, frightened things run from fire
and are torn apart, entrails devoured
first. The creature an ecstasy
of destruction and desire
Our way not quiet or kind
Even now, searching as I run
it runs, eyes foraging

I fast. In a little corner
with a little book, to live content
with just enough!
But the walls will not stay tight
Sounds enter and water seeps, forcing

me to listen and live on tiptoe
The walls float apart
on little waves
and swift, deep currents
carry me away
I reach to all the ones I love
who rush past me
blowing kisses, waving goodbye
Nothing I do can save them
Nothing can save me
from the terror of their beauty

Now in the cave, someone
stands before a fire
holding a knife
With a moan, he carves
his chest and lifts his heart
offers it to the fire
singing as it burns
swaying as the fire sways
laughing as the fire snaps
Mouthing sounds I cannot understand
he turns to me
I see the fire burning in his eyes
I see the flame behind him
I see            I see!
They are the same, the same!

*Lynn Hoggard*

## Kaleidoscope in White

*White is at the intersection of blue
and green and yellow and red . . . The
thrust must go through to the white.*
—W. C. Williams

Colors come to life before my eyes
and sing a soul in rhythm-colored tune:
kaleidoscopic dancing through the skies!

A yellow sun draws others where it lies
to splash them spinning wide again, and soon
their colors come to life before my eyes!

A few green leaves close-folded in disguise
unfurl into a parasol of bloom—
kaleidoscopic dancing in the skies!

When rubied heart cracks open like a cry
and purple tones go tilting into gloom
then colors come to life before my eyes

and call and call my song. Though body dies
some swirling, blue-flecked winter afternoon,
kaleidoscopic dancing of the skies,

a rainbow shimmers on until it guides
a sod of sound to swell before the moon
and a white song leaps before my eyes—
kaleidoscopic—dancing through the skies!

Laura Kennelly edits *Grasslands Review* and teaches English at the University of North Texas in Denton, Texas. Her chapbook, *The Passage of Mrs. Jung,* was published by Norton Coker Press (1990).

# Delta Ladies

Rain.
　Living, wetland, green shade, daydark, pouring rain—
　"Or a splash of bourbon?" In cool white-painted houses,
Delta ladies all their own wove word worlds. The girl child
listened.
　*"Ladies*, never *women*—make no mistake, heah?" her
mother told her. "Mississippi isn't Texas." Visits filled with rain
days dusting, polishing silver, smelling okra cooking, eating grits
and cheese, placing food—not in cool dining rooms watched over
by tiny jade deer nesting in waxy magnolia blooms on the
white-draped table—but in hot scented kitchens' Blue Willow
china, plastic red and white cloths punctuated by Lea & Perrins
and Avery Island's Tabasco handy. And hot tamales made with
stringy meat inside bought one street over one thousand miles
over since nobody was white.
　Rainy afternoons on screened-in porches, blown by
oscillating, ceiling fans, talking, drinking Coca-Cola,
wondering—did Beezle's boy really have to marry that Johnson
girl and did Pearl know she looked like a sausage in her new
beige dress and hidden fingers girdle?
　And then nights in rooms rain sealed close. Still air no fan
could shatter. Think of sleep. Think of breathing. Think of levees
breaking. Grandfather said the River touching the porch in
1934—even the houses looking like ladies—foundation skirts
lifting out of the muck—ignoring drowned Bossy and Caddie's
chicks and mud and sticks swirling, boiling at the steps' top.
　But now, it's got to be the rain. Unless it's the bourbon.
　Aunt Lucy, pastel print-dressed, soft, talcumed, almost
whispering "Drinking Coca-Cola out of a bottle is common, don't
you think, honey? Here, let me get you some ice for your glass.
No, don't get up. I'll freshen mine too."
　She did.
　And it wasn't always the bourbon inside the ladies. Husbands
always drank too much said the sugared voices on the dark
porches. "I mean, honey, you can tell he's had a little nip before

Sunday service. Course he's the salt of the earth and wouldn't hurt a fly. But still, remember Uncle Lester?—Fell off the dock and drowned.—And Aunt Leona?—never even knew where he hid the bottle."

Even now, I float; the liquid Delta lingers in my blood.

## Pre-Op

For you I will take off
clothes, rings, consciousness
and go into the dark.

Silent, I will lie on
a slab open to be
examined and altered.

Such frail flesh hides bones, holds
hormones tightly bound, laced
in blood, in secretions
driving desire, loosening
life—

Alone,
I might float forever
in that dark tunnel, travel
through one black night to the next.
But you make escape seem
cowardice, love seem all—

And a shared sunrise
worth the sharpest cut.

## Flash Flood

When you marry you wear
a ring and they never
tell you how strong
feeling can be.

Creek beds parch, unused
ninety-nine years,
but on that hundredth
we know why
they exist.

It doesn't rain much at first,
just a mist.

Then suddenly, in
an hour:

enough to sweep you
downstream, holding on
to nothing but air,
tumbling
while you wonder
if the ring
if the banks
will hold.

It's been that way
forever,
but no one remembers
to tell.

## Esperar lo imposible

Love inexorably alters my world; would
it could not.  Yet still my body reaches,
searches each morning for yours.  If I could
stop spring's onslaught, push buds back in branches
stifle the blue jay's courtship melodies—
so awkward, not summer's "cat, cat, cat"—
cut out each blossoming pear's memories
of fruition's ripe consequences that
never halt; lay waste to fertilities'
incessant clamor that I assent, give
homage to spring, love's possibilities,
then love might die, no nectar in my sieve.
But a world turned cold, turned clear without you
would lie, would cause this poem to be untrue.

## Testament

I am not Jacob, but I would
you would wrestle with me.  I could
pin you down, press
shoulders to ground
hands holding hard,
knees braced on your chest
my face, sweating, next
to yours, sweating too;
in my nostrils your
scent, shared breaths.

I would I could hold fast
until you cried why or how or
that you were sorry.

That's fair.

You have to be sorry for once;
either then or now.
I would I could hold you until
you say when.

## Hamlets

Every time it rains
tragedy at the
golf course pond.
Fingerlings flood caught
spill into great
adventures down the
gully to the Elm Fork.
They must move
quickly, taking water at
its flood or
it's too late.

This morning eight vibrated
in the diminishing current,
hesitating, fearing adventure,
yearning for home.

Fools, I wanted to shout,
take it while you can.

## Helen With Insomnia, at the Clavier

Paris was not the first. Did you think he was?
   How quaint.
There was Agamemnon, yes. His own brother.
At my wedding feast he fondled my breasts,
laughed, called my husband a lucky man.
After a while resisting seemed more
trouble than it was worth.
He loved me. But loved her, Clytemnestra, too.
   He said.
I think he loved power rich life more.
But his was a nasty family: ate each other.
That he didn't carry me off was all right.

It was less all right with Odysseus. No one
ever dreamed that when I walked long walks at
night I did not walk alone. No one ever saw
how we twined and tangled and became one,
startling night birds from the trees we sported
under. His stories, his laugh, his lips I could
have hung on forever.
   But he
was a hearth lover too. Stuck on status quo:
There she sat, always patiently waiting, lovely
Penelope. Slight smile on her perfect face—Oh,
I excited him more, but he's really a
coward—don't you know—it would have broken his
dear wife's heart and ruined
   his boy.

By the time Paris came, I was more than ready.
It's boring, you know, to be an old man's toy.
Of course I jumped: A foreign city, passionate
lover. (I never thought, then, to wonder why he
was so experienced, so knowing.) Yes I went
   with him.

Yet now he wanders from me and
the battlefield, chasing women, fleeing
slaughter, crying "Mama"
till she sweeps him to safety in a golden mist.

And the only real man here is tied to
Andromache.  I've seen the looks he gives me—
A man like that knows how to love his wife—
which (don't laugh) means
I can never have him.
But just once, I'd like to strip that plumed
helmet off his head, loosen the armor plate,
touch his skin and bring him to fevers,
feel his sweat dripping on
my body stretched beneath his—

And, yes, it's too bad about the war,
unfortunate, really—
but Aphrodite, after all, is not Athena.
Love cannot be expected to think
about everything.

## Clytemnestra Junior in Detroit

*"Police announced Tuesday Riggs' widow, Toni Cato Riggs,
22, and her brother Michael Cato, 19, had been charged with
first-degree murder in the slaying of the Patriot missile
crewman. Friends look to insurance money as the motive."*
USA Today 27 March 1991.

Bad news is always the same; only a few changes
in a few thousand years.

"New twist is no surprise to family, friends."

> Caught in a web
> He wasn't a king.
> She's not a queen,
> it was her brother,
> not his.

We enter this spectral city through concrete
tunnels engineered so tourists see no poor.

> She live by herself, she say.
> Girl, you believe that?

No beacons, no fires, announced Anthony Riggs home
bound. Fiberoptics, satellites spread the tidings.

> So she know. She
> prepare the happy
> homecoming.

When the police questioned us, we said:
"Start with the wife. She's the only one who has a motive."

> She all excited when he called up.
> Maybe he be gone ten years or
> come back dead.

Ole Clytemnestra, down on Elm street,
her man, he gone ten
years; when he get back,
he come down dead sure.

We weren't surprised:
"Start with the wife. She'll be a rich widow."

Anthony Riggs. He a good man.
Didn't tote no hussy home
no wall-eyed Cassie gal
talking silly to herself—
like the dead Agamemnon
over yonder on Elm street.

"I just hope it isn't true." Women become self-actualizing
when spouses absent themselves. We applaud opportunities
for personal development.

Oh that Toni, she empty
his bank account, wreck his
car in four months. Then she start
talking to her brother.
No, not his, hers.

Events such as this do tend to disillusion. Car dealers say
she'll get no sympathy car now. "I just hope it isn't true. I
hope that life hasn't come to mean nothing at all."

She seeing a shrink now. She
say all families dysfunctional at one time
or another.

## Lara to Zhivago

I have lived buried in flesh
and suns have risen to light
the love I had been longing
for. Once met, no room for fear,
free as infants we found feast,
nurtured fair words and fine love.

Now expensive conscience love
limits, confines to spirit; shuns flesh—
engages not in carnal feast.
And in winter's coldest light
whirls in unextinguished fear
undissolved by strong longing.

January's cold skies cover longing.
Sharp, snow-scattered shards love
shuns that knows no fear
save splitting soul from flesh
and forcing dark where light
might surprise, supply a feast.

Would we could celebrate a feast—
that loosening, releasing longing
when body touches body in the light,
rehearsing ancient rites with love
whose priests delight in flesh,
speak the truth of love, not fear.

Fallen, frozen lives may fear
release to pleasure, feast
that comes when flesh meets flesh.

In this Pauline kingdom, we are longing
not for despair; we are seeking richest Love
overall showering sparkling light.

*Laura Kennelly*

And thus it is that splendid spring light
burns away; forsakes cold winter fear;
grants patience with my weary love,
winter starved, afraid of feast,
of comfort, a baby—longing
return to warm, secret flesh.

My love, do not fear-light flesh
or fear generation's light-longing.
Hold me so souls may finely feast.

## Yard Report

Rain.
Last week four inches in an hour
frog-strangler gully washer.
It knocked the vinca
flat on their fannies,
but the watermelons
smacked their lips.

Today
Mosquitoes so fill the air
that
robins hopping through
grass with open mouths
have full bellies.

Vicky Lee Santiesteban received a bachelor's degree from St. Thomas University in Miami, Florida and has done graduate work in creative writing at the University of North Texas.

# Sightings

Like any normal kid, I wanted to go home.
I even acted sick, held my sun-burned stomach
in one hand and said I was going to puke
if we didn't leave soon. My dad just gave me
the keys to the car and said wait. For thirty
minutes I sat there listening to the radio, alone.

You shouldn't trust me—this was a long time ago—
but I think everyone made it out of the lake
except the driver. He landed the car in a cake
of mud and wouldn't give up the wheel, instead
he gripped with his legs refusing to be led,
and with his fists threw remarkably tough blows.

By the time the paramedics arrived, the car's
front-end was tipped forward, the grill kissing water.
Even though I wouldn't look, when I heard my father
say *oh my god*, I twisted the keys back and listened.
I still count that act as the greatest of my sins—
that moment I became one of the crowd's liars.

The falling away, the stupid sound that splash made
was silenced by an *ahh*, an *ahh* for fireworks
or grand prizes, and *ahh* so expectant it hurts,
and *ahh* for when something fascinating happens,
an *ahh* just deep and harsh enough that it deafens,
defines, makes sense of violent hungers unnamed.

All the way home, my mother talked about a tick,
a strange movement the driver made when they tried
to save him—as if he wanted to be revived.
I rolled down my window, pressed my head in the seat.
I burped and the taste of my acids was sweet.
Nothing was a game anymore. I really was sick.

II.

Imagine 9 a.m. in a suburban
neighborhood—imagine housewives and pre-schoolers
those artificers, or if you will, rulers
of the morning, bathed in red and blue flashing lights,
wearing shorts or flesh-tone, knee-high hose so tight
their calves fold and bulge like cottage cheese. Disturbed?

No, wait—that's nothing compared to the *real* tale:
two boys, skipping school, throwing rocks at canal cans
see something strange and make bets on their little hands,
who's got the best aim, what the hell they're aiming for
and one won or lost—this depends on who keeps score—
because his rock hit dead-on and up popped a swollen male.

A television crew films the excavation.
A flowered woman comes forward and reports
that she heard the shots and thought they were fireworks.
Later, the police pull her aside for questioning.
She goes, half under her breath mentioning
there's coffee at her house—a stiff invitation.

When they got the body up, no one made a sound;
the noise of the separation was loud enough—
the thick sucking tonus of his body, the tough
draw of stale water letting him finally go,
a mechanical mouth snapping shut and the show
ended when everyone knew what it looks like to drown.

Someone mentioned tragedy as if it fit this stage.
It was a long time before anyone had strength
enough to go home and clean their toilets, angst
biting the backs of their thongs and fuzzy slippers.
One woman took to her gardenias with blunt clippers
while our two young heroes cried in their mothers' legs.

III.

You can lose the things you love a lot of ways.
That's what makes this life so goddammed interesting.
But what's even better is you can keep guessing.
Say a good friend disappears one day, just like that,
like some well-trained magician slipped her in his hat
when no one was looking. You'd have to be amazed.

But no one knows her. There's nothing dramatic;
it's an austere disappearance, for instance
an appointment she had to keep, a circumstance
beyond her control, so she misses dinner
and you'll call anyone, wondering if they've seen her.
Hey, trust me: you were made just right for this, thick.

No, it's not the simple things that will bother you.
It's not even the strange ones, or the violent
mistakes made when no one seems to be intent
on troubling you. Just hope you'll get to be
one of the watchers, or the watched—you'll see
how entirely entertaining it is. And true.

Make up stories about what happened to your friend.
Why waste her life on some casual mistake?
Why, you can even videotape the well-caked
newscastress when she mispronounces the name, again.
Be offended, write letters to the station, demand
that they get it right. Tell them you're gonna suspend

*everything* until there's some formal apology
made to you because you are someone in all
of this—say it's not fair because you waited a long
time to be on the other side of the story,
on the side that knows no answer will worry
you so long as somebody marvels your suffering.

## The Seraphs of Spain

Antonio picks grapes in the South of France.
Four summers now he has felt the juice of delusion
dripping down his forearms, ambitiously riding
through the maze of curled black hair there
and falling in tiny, sweet drops upon the earth.

He has a friend who speaks patterned English—
whose eyes are romantic and punctuate
his broken dialogue. We drink stale, flat beer
and Antonio has his like water. Little words
in drunken tongue stains the rims of our mugs.

The two men dance the serviana while I watch.
Antonio's angry feet pound into the still
afternoon siesta.  When the music ends, the friend
bows backwards and Antonio kisses him on the mouth
looking at me as if he hopes I will be offended.

That night, we find a park in the Ronda hills—
our cliff is carved deep and *the bridge has killed men*,
the friend tells me. Antonio is restless,
he interrupts, his voice echoing, moving
beyond the three of us and into the gorge.

*Era loco edificar una puente como aquella*,
Antonio shouts, spitting smoke and throwing
his cigarette out into nothing. I watch it
catch rocks, tenuous sparks battling the wind.
The beer in me anticipates a fire in the brush.

I sleep on the train ride back to Madrid and dream
I am on my knees in a vineyard when a dark haired
angel lets a slow trickle of wine wash over my face,
warming my neck, and I am drunk with excitement
knowing that later I will digest him.

## Tatoos, Other Information

The pages of your letter smelled like skin
and there was a strand of your dark brown hair
in the crease of page three. Then your tattoo—
how you must have scribbled, erased, revised.
I suppose I should tell you I cried.

Oh, there were things that should have had their impact—
Vinnie's new show, leaving the old college,
the bacteria that choked your goldfish
and how you froze their little orange and green
bodies that they might suffer less. Funny.

Then in the midst of living your life
you had your wrist carved. You were altered.
I wonder about that alien landscape
etched in deep red and black—painful
exhilaration you called it—and I need to know,

when the artist's needle made its first
delicate puncture, did you feel anything enter?
Did you realize a subtle escape?
Now these possibilities make you strange.
I always thought your wrist was lovely enough.

Perhaps now I would find it beautiful
when you rest your brown haired head on your hand
and those new lines about you catch light.

## Pan

From the Cuban bakery we'd buy bread.
*Pan por favor.* Pooling fifty cents
between us, handing it to the baker's wife,
trying to make an exit before **he**
would come—the man with *los ojos grandes.*
He knew when we were there, sniffed us out
over the smell of cinnamon and yeast.
He'd hold a tray of pastries or cookies
covered in tiny, colored, candied beads.
*Tu quieres?* Latin lines for little girls.
*No gracias*, we'd mumble, avoiding his gaze—
wait until the door closed him behind us
before calling against his advances, *Maricon.*
Over the burning asphalt we'd dash
to our shaded dining room with the insects.
Peeling the crust, we'd punch into moistness,
roll the white innards into firm balls,
popping them into our mouths. Brown, crisp flakes
fell around us. The baker would watch,
paunched belly curving the wind around him,
his eyes concentrated on our chewing.
We'd stay just until the red ants attacked,
stinging our bare legs in savage hunger.
The welts they left turned red with our scratching.
Those times, we misunderstood too much—thought
nothing of spit soothing our infections,
rubbing our young thighs with wetted fingers
while the *Maricon* tended to his rising loaves.

# My Babylon

I had the sort of fever that made the walls breathe, and the dolls on their pedestals—I knew they were desperate to dance over the edge—their plastic toes pointed. I was close to sleeping; denying the disease, falling off for a while. But when I sensed him coming down the hall, carrying a small paper umbrella or a go-go can or some stupid gift from the beachside restaurant where he worked, my determination to be ill intensified. Oh, Papa. Oh, my pretty Papa. Make me good.

He lay beside me, blew lightly on my face to spread the stray hairs of my bangs back. I knew then that he would never be angry with me for succumbing to such wilds, that the rains were too warm, that I had strange fascinations. I counted the pocks in his face. I told him to hum while I played with his lower lip. *I promise you a chestnut.* Please Papa. *You will always be beautiful.* Oh Papa. *Go now. Sleep.* I never felt him leave my bed. I'll never understand how he could.

I was often just that sick. It was either the children who rubbed mud in my hair or the neighborhood ghosts or seeing a car catch the back of my dog. Sometimes, I was so simple even my knees would ache. Anything. Anything real. Not one bit of it was created. I didn't mean to frighten him. I only knew too much to ever want to leave my bed. It was easier there. Still, the dark was a cruel place to keep me. He must have know known that. I said it so many times.

## Three Invariable Stories:

A Ride

You are on a brown pony-horse just the right size for your adolescent thighs to hold tight without tiring. Your hair is the same color as the horse's mane and you ride slow. You wonder who makes these trails, maybe some invisible trail maker, a ghost with a sharp machete clips branches in places you are afraid to put your own feet. You think, "The trees and grass grow behind me. Maybe I won't ever go back." You find a clearing, branches grown over like a dome of swift greenery, a small space, just small enough for you and your horse to pass. You need only duck your head. Twigs tangle your hair, strands of you remain in the trees. A clearing as spacious as any young mind might allow, light coming through in rushes, a light steady enough for an imaginative child. And you see. You see where butterflies are born, where butterflies test their painted wings, hundreds of butterflies in a clearing colored by shade, colored by the sun through leaves, until everything is a muted green, your skin, your horse, the rich ground on which you stand. Only the butterflies have color. You breathe butterfly air. Their beating wings breed silence, an emptiness of sound, a hush that was never hushed. You stand still for a very long time. This is the closest you will ever come to life or death with no commitment to either. You ride home to tell a story no one believes, your heels flogging the gut of your horse, and because you tried to give this place away with words, it never comes again.

The Wind

My grandmother came to me. I was in my car, driving through a storm, and she said, "Listen to the wind." I thought *How odd. Listen to the wind.* And then I heard it. I heard a wind both frightening and soothing and wanted to listen, thought listening would be the most pleasant thing to do, but at the same time knew the wind would kill me. I couldn't breathe. *This was a dream.* I'm telling you because I want you to know how it was. I want you to know how I never met my grandmother, how she died when I was five. Once a neighbor came to me and asked, "How is your grandmother?" I was wearing a pretty dress that floated when I spun, so I spun, my dress floated and I said, "Guess." I thought how pretty and important I was to have an invisible grandmother and at the same time have a dress that floated when I spun. But it's not really about wind that I'm telling you. And it's not even about my grandmother, how she was spinning and floating, lost to me somehow. Listen.


Heat Lightning

is silent, a temporary scar of light on our darkness, a temporal darkness invading our light. We turn off the car radio, roll down the windows, as if there were something to hear. A welcoming flash of light in the distance, we head in its direction. It does not move and we drive faster, laughing. We will get up under it. We've found the end of our rainbow and it's made of electricity. Hurry. We park along the bay line, snap three photographs, quick, hope to catch something. Nothing in the world moves but us and the sky. We are generators of light, light our conduit. We watch a fish jump from water to air. Listen. Nothing sounds wrong.

Sheryl St. Germain earned degrees from Southeastern Louisiana University and the University of Texas at Dallas. She now teaches English at Knox College, Galesburg, Illinois. Her most recent publication is *How Heavy the Breath of God* (University of North Texas Press, 1994).

# Dallas Texas: Not From a Native Daughter

I've almost gotten used to the accent, although
the native male still sounds like he's got a half-
ate boiled egg in his mouth when he talks; the words
are never chewed enough, like the land itself they are
half digested, the words can't say all he wants them
to say, it's as if he wants them to be as big and unruly
as his belly, his woman, his state; everyone overstuffs
the words with syllables so that some are always
falling out of their mouths. The natives here
are not unlike their favorite condiment: barbecue
sauce—slow and sloppy, tart and rich, thick-bodied,
smoked with pride at being just this: a Texan.

Many who live in Dallas are not Texans, not all women
are tight-jeaned and wide-hipped, big-busted and over-
flowing with body like the land, the sauce and the accent.
Not all men are Bible-belted and preachy, or gun-toting,
pick-up-truck-driving and tobacco-chewing. Many of us
are here, so we say, from other places we love better—
Louisiana, Arkansas, Alabama, Mississippi.

We have come here for work, we have come to this amorphous,
spread-out land, this land that not even a public transportation
system can keep gridded together, this cultureless, face-
less land, and we stay, we say, out of necessity, not
out of love, we stay despite the embarrassment of living here,
the utter ridiculousness of downtown Dallas that over spills
itself, the buildings, like the words trying to say more
than is possible:

       the Green building, its garish cartoon
outline visible a hundred miles on a clear night;
the ball of the Hyatt that on bad nights looks like
a Martian ship on drugs, the lights blinking on and off,
hundreds of them, with no apparent pattern; the building
that looks like a cigarette lighter waiting for some great

hand to split the sky and flick it on; and the one with
Pegasus flying on top (only in Dallas could the connection
be made between the son of Medusa and the selling of oil and gas);
and the building with the X stretched in lights all across it
like some dire punishment or mark of treasure; and now
the female building that has a hole in it, as if
to defy and tempt the manly sky scrapers that surround it
to turn sideways and enter it (only in Dallas could the
connection be made between buildings and sex).

But it is this, if truth be told, that keeps us here,
not that the lemon blue sky, as unending as milk, is not
tempting, or the clusters of mesquite, or the flowering
in spring and summer, but maybe there is something stubborn
and American about this unshapeliness, this bounty, this
half-digested wisdom, the fearless stupid intelligence
that believes anything to be possible: again, the frontier.

# In the Garden of Eden

No one tells much about it,
but there were vultures in the Garden of Eden.
Turkey vultures, to be exact.
Dark eagles, they would soar like gods,
voiceless, their wings held out in blessing,
their unfeathered heads the red-jewels
of the sky of the garden.

They were vegetarian then.
There were no roadside kills,
no bones to pick, no dead flesh to bloom, ripen.

And they were happy.
They could not imagine
what they would become.

## Sestina to the Beloved

I would wake at night to the breath,
the sound of them together, their want,
the smell of their thighs and bones,
even thousands of miles away I could feel him undress
her, could hear his voice speaking
her name, it is not my name, which is difficult.

What he had with the two of us was not difficult,
it was as easy as night's breath,
as easy as me not speaking,
not saying what it was I wanted
most, not saying I wanted to undress
only for one man, only for one to know the bones

of me, the bones of my mouth, the bones
of my feet, of my heart, even the difficult
bones of my face and hands, my eyes and sex, only one to undress
my voice, only one to sing my breath,
only one to know the forest of my want,
to know there is only one who is speaking

my name in dreams, speaking
my body as if even voice had bones.
What I want is uncompromising, what I want
is difficult,
is like wanting water to offer breath,
is like wanting fire to undress

itself, is about possession undressing
itself, is about what it means to be speaking
at all, is about belonging like breath
to the beloved, the one whose bones
are inside you like so many difficult
hearts, the only one you want to want

so much that all there is of living is that want.
I cannot tell you it will be easy to undress
your heart only for me, that I will not be difficult,
that some days and nights you may feel as if you are speaking
to no one, that some nights your bones
won't ache for the touch of another, the sweet breath

of the unknown, the undressed breath
of one less difficult, a bone-
want that I will recognize, whose ache I will honor and sweeten
   with my love, my many, many breaths.

## My Body in Summer

Not yet calloused, but cut and scarred,
bruised and dirty because I don't
wear gloves, am ungraceful—

I smell like sun, wine,
unstable weather, heavy rains,
peppers from the garden,
grass, new paint, like labor,
sadness, like a mother
who has lost her child,
weeds, tomato vine
ready to break from
the weight of tomatoes,

like broken
fingernails, finger
crescents of dirt, sex
without sex, like when a woman
removes her diaphragm
and smells the mushroom
smell of the gone one,

coconut, ink, despair, fern,
skin-grit, bruises, black flies,
who love my skin, it is a banquet
with its small wounds,
its salt and wine and smoke
smell from the barbecue,
my pungent armpits, fertile
as any forest,
sphagnum moss,
soft rotting wood,
the way river birches bend
until I think I will die of their beauty,

smell of everything I have touched
intimately and everything I have wanted to,
red biting ants, blood mosquitoes,
insect bodies that go flat like love
when we smash them,
all the small terrors we smell of,
hand of beloved,
milk, music and sky,
hope and veins, I am a feast,
a garden, a corpse,
my skin sucked and flayed,

and the late sun's death,
thick and creamy and dark,
covers my skin like a sauce:

from this have you come,
to this shall you return,
take this and eat of it,
this odoriferous perfume,
this blessed sweating body.

## At Paisano, Thinking About How We End Things

This: to name the thing between us
that our bodies know and will not touch.
Fanged snake I have not yet seen,
bone of deer, skin-bleached.
Absence of storms.
Sun that strips the porch clean of night.
My face dredged from the creek today,
horribly aged.

The nameless thing blisters between us.
I offer poems, trinkets that are not enough.
You present your fear, which I cannot cure.

I will get an animal for the nights.
A truck, maybe a gun.

## Pain Killers

I love those drugs they give
to relax you, the kind gas
of the dentist, the mysterious
pills and shots before and after
surgery, you lie there
on the chair or the bed
like Christ, all your wounds
illuminated, vibrating
with existence:

                        for this is what
those drugs do, they do not
kill pain,  they illuminate it,
fertilize it, until you are
so aware that you are almost
numb, it is pain made so much
itself it doesn't seem like itself.

So there you are in the chair
thinking *I must cut the grass*
*I must clean the house I*
*must read important books*
*and underline the important*
*parts,* and then the drug
kicks in its sweetness

and your wrists that had been
tight with trouble, your wrists
that had shouted and shook
at your child, begin to warm and blush

and your body relaxes. You lie there
like nothing, the pathways
to memory opening, you can feel
the doors opening in all the veins
of your body, the first touch,

the first disappointment,
now you can stand to think
about it, now you can remember it,
despair, bitterness fully remembered,
fully clothed, sweet grace,
you hold it in your body,
try to make it last,
close your eyes

and remember

how your brother would take
this sweetness, how he took it
and took it until his eyes closed.

Our eyes do not close like his. We
are lying down in an office, we
are waiting for a dentist, a surgeon
to cut us open, deliver us.

# Death, on Vacation, Tends Her Garden

I love that greening in spring in the mouth of the sun,
the way the earth sings here, not dark but green
with me. And the bees, the way they separate
the petals of flowers
with such gentleness and sureness,
what I would give
to have a beloved like a bee!
To love like that
I would die myself.

And I love the way seeds
break open in the earth unseen
and breathe themselves
into air, the way leaves unfurl
like flags from young stems weak
as mortal lives, I could break them
with a hard rain,

the way they are like human lips,
those first leaves opening,
and I love the way the weeds cry tragically
to get in, as relations at funerals,

flowers, like lipsticked nipples,
the stout herbs with their fragrances
that come from being bruised,
I love them too,
the way grief turns to scent,
the way regret becomes soil,
black loam—

here I am loved, here am I love,
here are my voices, eyes, mouths
skins, here, the place I betray
what I am.

## Keeping the Roses Alive

1

The rose bushes were not mine,
never would I have planted such clichés
of daintiness and fragility, cultivated
so long for beauty that they had
lost all hope of strength.
But I decided to try to keep them alive.

I am a twenty-four hour nurse,
and they are my patients
sick and yellowed, but still living.

No other plant has so many enemies:
rose aphids, rose gall, rose chafers,
rose midges, rose scales, rose slugs,
rose stem borers, rose weevils;
Japanese beetles, red spider
mites, bronzing, brown canker, stem
canker, leaf rust, powdery mildew,
crown cell, innumerable nasty viruses,
and finally, black spot,
which can't be cured, although the books
say prevention with fungicide is possible:
cut off all the infected leaves, spray
on a weekly basis every bit of the rest
of the bush, don't forget under the leaves.

2

It must have been one mad cell
we didn't get, the doctor tells me.
Pruning the breasts is not always
100 percent effective. The two lumps,
black as black spot, in the lymph
glands, inoperable.

Later, I call myself up on the phone
to say how sorry I am to hear.
Doctors say six, maybe eight months
I tell me. My voice is slurred,
but numbly happy. I have
started drinking again, I say.
I will not undergo the fungicide,
I say. *I understand*, I say,
*I would do the same.*

This morning the rose buses
pushed me too far. I drank
a coffee cup of bourbon,
pulled the fuckers up
by the roots.

## Hacking Away the Wisteria

The wisteria had become wanton, exuberant,
triumphant, almost hysterical, breathing its way across my mother's
lawn, working its way underneath the shed through the
floor, willing itself through the ceiling and out the
window, to the holly tree on the other side of the yard,
wrapping itself around everything in its way, the azaleas,
hibiscus, camellias, all caught in its stranglehold,
insidious, another summer neglected and it would
enter the house, sneak its green fingers into my
mother's bedroom, surround her body while she
slept, enter her like some ancient god,

or my father—
*We planted it together long ago*, she says.
*See how it poisons the ground,* she says.

She had tried to kill it several
times, deciding she didn't want it
after it responded too well to the climate,
frightened her, like a child gone wild
with its willful living, *it's like a thing
from out of space,* she tells me,
and I see she is frightened,
she is thinking about her death;
every time I visit she gives me
something from my childhood,
tells me about some thing I need
to know for when she dies.

So I become the kind of son
she never had, a noble prince, the hacksaw
my sword. I set to, hacking away at
the wisteria. I make a big deal of it, the way
we always make much of something
easy enough to do, so that
it counts in our favor when the harder thing,
which we cannot do, comes up.

*How much, how much*
*do you have to cut off to begin again*
*in that dark moist place of terror*
*and beauty, would we ever do it*
*if we knew what we nurtured*
*would become weed—*

Afterwards, I place a piece of it
with root in a pot. When I leave,
the wisteria hacked down,
I take it home with me,
plant it in my yard.

I plant it
as if it were a piece of my mother,
as if it were a piece of my father,
as if it were my mother's slow death,
my father's gangrenous leg, his shriveled liver,
and I watch daily to see
if it's taken root,
I imagine it in my dreams,
the first push of new root into
soft fresh soil, moist with waiting, *wildness,*

*wisdom, weeping, wickedness,*
*word, woman, wish, welt, wailing,*
*wanting, withdrawing, wet, within,*
*whip, willful, willing, wind* there is

no wisteria in me, no wisteria,
there is nothing
my son will have to hack out.

Frances M. Treviño is pursuing her teaching certification in English at St. Mary's University in San Antonio, Texas. She works for the San Antonio Independent School District.

# I Am a Mexican Who Looks Jewish

I am a Mexican who looks Jewish
with orange hair
and hazel eyes
white skin—
not brown.

I am a Mexican living
in the United States—
third generation Texan
and first generation
not to speak
the language of my
parents and grandparents.

I ask my mother,
after growing up with
mariachi music,
Vincente Fernandez,
and Los Tres Panchos
in my grandmother's
candled house,
I ask her what music
was her favorite?
and she replies—
"Motown."

I realize something is lost.

And in the small
family streets of
Pharr, Tx,
my father struggles
for his college degree
and eventually embraces
middle management,
and happily forgets

the small streets
of Pharr and
the culture that bound him.

No language,
no music,
no poetry,
no memory,
no mexicans
in our house.

Despite the names
Maria, Carmen, Rosa,
Esparanza, Maragarita,
Teresa, Luis, Enrique,
Imelda, Irene, and Juan—

my father's eleven
brothers and sister.

But me,
I have my grandmother's
name, and she has her
grandmother's name
and I have the memories
and I was the one
in a family
of güeras,
born with
a brown soul.

*Frances M. Treviño*

# To You Who Leave San Antonio

*—for a friend moving to Maine*

You will remember San Antonio
Colored warm with stripes
Even the blues are orange
Missing the eastern draft
Eleven months out of the year
Nourishing the salt of a million tears
San Antonio humble servant
Not quite pre-columbian
You are the Spanish of a dark brown flavor
Scented like church and pecan

You will remember the dank humidity
Dark-skinned Indian faces
How close you were to the Mexican border
And how you boardered so close to Mexicans

You will remember the enchiladas and guacamole
The gorditas and salsitas
Food so foreign you won't forget too soon
And you will remember the tortilla moon
Those rolled words you couldn't pronounce
The tongue that won't cooperate—
tortillaria, huaraches, chorizo—
Spicy words that seem absurd

You will remember San Antonio
Dusty and hot-breezed
The orange and pink threaded South Texas horizon
Weaving you back to the East

## My Mother Who Burns Tortillas

*Not all women who are married*
*should wife.*

*And it is rumored that kitchens*
*are happier with good cooks.*

It is Sunday with little or no exception
when my mother decides to cook.

She strolls in chanclas
across the tile, cool and clay,
and opens the refrigerator door.
She removes the eggs, bacon, sausage,
and a package of twenty C&C Bakery tortillas.

As she cracks the eggs and scrambles
the yellow paste, I can almost taste
the smell of burnt tortillas.

She flicks it onto the black, spiral burner,
set at level seven, and gathers the plates,
blue and speckled.
Holding them, she walks to the table
and places one at each wooden chair.

The poor tortilla, being subjected
to level seven heat, begins to blacken.

She walks to the rooms of my
brother and sister and calls them
to the table.

The poor tortilla, now with a
black, spiral scar, begins to smoke.

My mother shuffles back to the kitchen,
"Damn" she says, flips it over and whispers
"It's still good" under her breath.

Last Sunday she went outside to get the paper
and found an interesting article.
Before that it was something with the dog.
And without fail, the phone rings
as the tortilla sits and burns.

## Cabrona

sips sweet sangria
purses her lips
to savor
the little bit of sour
and orders new pitchers
by the hour
tells me
girlfriend—
don't pretend
lookin like
you wanna be me
she spins in the middle
of moustached mariachis
shakes herself
fine like that
they tell her
andale mujer
one more time

# Woman at Twenty-Eight

*—for Cindy*

we have shared
the deep cut red
of opinionated lips
have spoken our
minds on occasion
and like the strength
of ancient egyptian
women have fought
and won the battles
of drowning men

Yours is a rusty brilliance
October gold leaf
Autumn refreshment
Scented like almond vanilla
Lemon grapefruit rind
Solemn spiced splendor

Tender wicked virgin
South Texas neighborhood beauty
Ranch queen race car driver
Mother of quiet virtue
You are an architect of nourishment
Bacon bean mixture of
Backyard gatherings
Daughter dancing on clouds

We have not shared wine
But whispered while
In a kitchen confessional
Laughing at mistakes
Buttering bread
Sweetening the tea
Kitchen with watermelon walls

*A Certain Attitude*

You adhere to a gentle glory
You an olive angel
Rising south to the Mexican sun

# San Antonio Southside Women

fling the knives
in jealous furies
at the unfaithful boyfriends
faithfully denying
such women exist

curse the mothers
who protect
the filthy lies

smear their tears
mascaraed black & raging

and hold the babies
who will love them
in the unconditional way
which their
boyfriends and husbands
do not

## Freddy Fender You Are a King

Dusty cowboy
Of the next tear drop

Lone Star confessions
Crooner of the valley

Low-ceiling cantina
Cold beer in a bottle

Sweating in summer
Summer strung over

Naked lightbulbs
On an extension cord wire

You are a wailer
Of love songs

Sung on a patio cafe
I have spun

Slow danced
In your reign

Torn into a lime
Sprinkled with salt

Tasted the southern
Nectar of lime and salt

Crying the mystical call
Of a brokenhearted culture

Like fog rising
Above the Rio Grande

## Southern and in Detroit

*—August 1993*

I do not like the empty buildings
in Detroit
cradled in the eerie whispers
of angry ghosts
rocking in the river breezes
white and smoke-stacked

Even the pigeons
look industrial
crooked and hard.

There is a quiet muck of activity
and a slight drizzle
and I wish it were 1955
in Detroit
now the raging voices gone
engines dead and rusting
barges humming along the river way
barges slow, tired, and achy

And now, more than ever
I think I miss the South.

## The Indian of My Dreams

He is the Indian of my dreams
My Aztec theatre
The crushed velvet muscle ripple
Of my tequila fantasies
Soft-spoken and caramel
He is feathered with raw regal splendor.

I want to gather my lips
And whisper temptation
Give him the look I reserve
Only for the finest of men
Imagine my hand combing the threads
Of his Indian hair
My teeth caught between the
Black beads of the necklace given to
Him by his other lover.
Briefly, I savor my weakness.

He is his mother's favorite angel.
Fifth child born with his
Grandmother's last blessing
Tragic ultimate good-bye
From his mother's mother.
Protected by the cross on
St. Anthony's shoulder that
He should only find happiness
This miracle baby whom I indulge.

He is my favorite devil
The red tongue in my olive
My final flirtation on a Thursday night
After I've swallowed my fill
On the last call
After Coyote Dreams have
Packed their guitars and symbols
He is the one I choose.

And if he can withstand
The wrath of my fire crown
Claws on my hands and feet
Badness in me
Then he can embrace the energy of
Any mountain, ocean or desert
And I would climb the pyramids of Tenochtitlan
Again and again and again
In honor of my worthy warrior.

## To You Who Sleep Somewhere in Texas

My love to you
You who sleep somewhere in Texas
Somewhere in a coolen painted sky
In the great north barren beauty
Away from the brown south
Chromed and low
Tomato chunked with onion

You with quiet broken hands
Healing praying playing
Into a pan handle nova
Mysterious Texas constellations
Staring at you staring at me
Colliding us to sleep
In the north and south of
Texas
Territory wide with dusty desert

And in the whirlwind of
Grain and salt
Where horizon and landscape
Mesh into the only
Texas sunsets in the world
Is me in the south
In the echoing mission
Of San Antonio
Loving you
Who sleep somewhere
In Texas.